Successful Career and Life Planning

The Systems Thinking Approach[SM]

Stephen G. Haines

A Fifty-Minute™ Series Book

> This Fifty-Minute™ book is designed to be "read with a pencil." It is an excellent workbook for self-study as well as classroom learning. All material is copyright-protected and cannot be duplicated without permission from the publisher. *Therefore, be sure to order a copy for every training participant by contacting:*
>
> 1-800-442-7477 • 25 Thomson Place, Boston MA • www.courseilt.com

Successful Career and Life Planning
The Systems Thinking Approach[SM]

Stephen G. Haines

with contributions by:
Partners and Associates of the Centre for Strategic Management®
Jayne Haines, Laurie Hyde, Frank Kurucz, Valerie MacLeod, Dennis Rowley, Gail Rowley

Credits:
Editor: **Brenda Pittsley**
Copy Editor: **Charlotte Bosarge**
Production Manager: **Judy Petry**
Cover: **Nicole Phillips**
Artwork: **Ralph Mapson**
Text Design: **Amy Shayne**
Production Artist: **Robin Strobel**

COPYRIGHT © 2000 Course Technology, a division of Thomson Learning. Thomson Learning is a trademark used herein under license.

ALL RIGHTS RESERVED. No part of this work may be reproduced, transcribed, or used in any form or by any means—graphic, electronic, or mechanical, including photocopying, recording, taping, Web distribution, or information storage and retrieval systems—without the prior written permission of the publisher.

For more information contact:

    Course Technology
    25 Thomson Place
    Boston, MA 02210

Or find us on the Web at **www.courseilt.com**

For permission to use material from this text or product, submit a request online at www.thomsonrights.com.

Trademarks
Crisp Learning is a trademark of Course Technology. Some of the product names and company names used in this book have been used for identification purposes only, and may be trademarks or registered trademarks of their respective manufacturers and sellers.

Disclaimer
Course Technology reserves the right to revise this publication and make changes from time to time in its content without notice.

ISBN 1-56052-562-2
Library of Congress Catalog Card Number 00-101081
Printed in Canada by Webcom Limited

3 4 5 PM 06 05 04

Learning Objectives For:

SUCCESSFUL CAREER AND LIFE PLANNING

The objectives for *Successful Career and Life Planning* are listed below. They have been developed to guide you, the reader, to the core issues covered in this book.

THE OBJECTIVES OF THIS BOOK ARE:

❑ 1) To provide a systematic approach for determining what you want out of life

❑ 2) To explain how to think backwards from your goals and plan how to achieve them

❑ 3) To help couples and families form a mutual vision for personal and professional success

❑ 4) To guide individuals and business partners through an annual process of reviewing and refining plans

ASSESSING YOUR PROGRESS

In addition to the learning objectives above, Course Technology has developed a Crisp Series **assessment** that covers the fundamental information presented in this book. A 25-item, multiple-choice and true/false questionnaire allows the reader to evaluate his or her comprehension of the subject matter. To buy the assessment and answer key, go to www.courseilt.com and search on the book title or via the assessment format, or call 1-800-442-7477.

Assessments should not be used in any employee selection process.

About the Author

Stephen G. Haines is an internationally recognized leader in the field of strategic management. His unique background includes extensive experience as a senior executive and board member for international and Fortune 500 firms. He has worked with eight top management teams, including two divisions at Marriott and MCI Communications Corporation. He has also conducted planning for many school districts, as well as with individuals, couples, and the members of many family-owned businesses.

In addition, Steve has been vice president of human resources and administration at Sun International Inc. (Sunoco); senior vice president of planning, human resources and administration at Freddie Mac; and executive vice president and chief administrative officer of Imperial Corporation of America, a financial services company with assets worth $13 billion. He also was chief executive officer and part-owner of the prestigious University Associates Consulting and Training Services. He is a 1968 graduate of the United States Naval Academy and a former Naval officer.

Steve is now the owner and founder of the Centre for Strategic Management, located in San Diego. Steve and his partners at the Centre for Strategic Management have conducted hundreds of strategic planning processes for businesses of all types including private, public, military, government, and family-owned, and associations throughout the United States, Europe, Asia, Canada, Australia, South America, and South Africa.

To receive a copy of their product catalog or more information about the Centre please contact:

Centre for Strategic Management • 1420 Monitor Road • San Diego, CA 92110
(619) 275-6528 or fax (619) 275-0324 • email: csmintl@san.rr.com
www.csmintl.com

Dedication

This book is dedicated to my clients who own family businesses. From them I have learned and continue to learn so much about families, love, life, and careers. It is also dedicated to children everywhere. If I could change only one thing in life, it would be to require children at all levels of schooling to practice strategic career and life planning to ensure they get the most life has to offer.

Steve Haines

To the Reader

> *"Life is an exciting business and most exciting when it is lived for others."*
>
> —Helen Keller

Welcome to *Successful Career and Life Planning*. This book is designed for you to write in, think about, and use over and over again. The self-paced format will allow you to read and work on the activities at your own pace—this book is not meant to be completed at one sitting. The goal is to help individuals, couples, families, and members of family-owned businesses practice successful life planning.

This book presents strategic career and life planning based on three common-sense premises. They are:

1. **Planning is integral to life.** Planning can shape careers and lives and help individuals or families achieve their life visions. Thus, planning is integral to a comprehensive Strategic Life Management System. It is a way to manage your life, your relationships, and your career. Planning means focusing on desired outcomes.

2. **People support what they help create.** Individuals and families who practice Strategic Career and Life Planning in an evolutionary and participatory way will generate critical support for the desired changes or outcomes

3. **Systems Thinking** provides the framework for this book. Systems Thinking starts with defining your desired future or end result. Keep this result in mind in all you plan and implement. Systems Thinking encourages a focus on outcomes and an ideal future vision, rather than on inputs or routine daily activities as the primary purpose in life.

In summary, this book has a goal of helping you to design, build, and sustain your life and career productively and successfully with a Strategic Career and Life Plan.

Contents

Introduction viii

Part 1: What Is Strategic Career and Life Planning?

Getting Started with Backward Thinking 3
Common-Sense Premise 1: Planning Is Integral to Life 4
Common-Sense Premise 2: People Support What They Help Create ... 6
Common-Sense Premise 3: Systems Thinking 8
Systems Thinking Approach—A New Orientation to Life 9

Part 2: Getting Ready to Plan: Setting the Stage

The Environment: Revolutionary and Global Changes 13
Plan-to-Plan: The Organizing and Tailoring Step 20
Identify Stakeholders 22
Decision-Making by Consensus 23
Potential Barriers 24

Part 3: The ABC Phases

Phase A: Output—Creating Your Ideal Future 31
Phase B: Feedback—Measuring Success 44
Phase C: Input—Developing and Converting Strategies into Action ... 50
Personal Annual Work Plan 63
Resource Allocation Plan 66

Part 4: Implementing Plans Successfully

Phase D: Throughput—Plan to Implement 71
Some Final Thoughts on Change 76
Two Keys to Success 79
Annual Strategic Reviews 84
Summary: A Challenge for the Future 85

Part 5: Appendix

Sample Strategic Career and Life Plan 88

Introduction

> *"A strong passion for any object will ensure success, for the desire of the end will point out the means."*
>
> —Ben Stein

Strategic Career and Life Planning is an underutilized concept. This book is designed to help you clarify what it is all about. It will help you to demystify terms. It also will give you a simple ABCD system to unlock the mysteries of Strategic Career and Life Planning and accomplish a successful plan.

Strategic Career and Life Planning is the place to start if you want to be successful and profitable. Many successful men and women of the world use their imaginations…they first think ahead to create a mental picture of the future. They then *"think backward"* to the present and go to work materializing that mental picture in all its details, filling in here, adding a little there, altering this a bit and that a bit, but steadily building—steadily building. This is backward thinking, which will be discussed throughout this book.

This book is organized into five parts:

Part 1 defines the concepts that will be presented as elements of Strategic Career and Life Planning. Parts 1 and 2 are intended to be read as pre-work (called "plan to plan") for the actual completion of your Strategic Career and Life Plan.

Part 2 looks at Strategic Career and Life Planning in light of revolutionary and global changes going on in the world today. It then looks at the implications of those changes as they relate to applications in individual careers and lives.

Part 3 is the heart of the book. This is where you develop the ABC phases of your Strategic Career and Life Plan using backward thinking. Begin by defining your ideal future, then think and work backward to that future.

Part 4 will assist you in the action planning that needs to be done once you have completed your Strategic Career and Life Plan. Part 4 walks you through a yearly project map to guide your changes and implementation. This map will help you use Strategic Career and Life Planning to manage your life and career.

Part 5 is an appendix that contains a sample Strategic Career and Life Plan.

PART 1

What Is Strategic Career and Life Planning?

> "*The greatest discovery in our lives is that human beings, by changing the inner attitudes of their minds, can change the outer aspects of their lives.*"
>
> —William James

2

Getting Started with Backward Thinking

This book operates from the assumption that you become more successful the moment you start moving toward a worthwhile goal. Strategic Career and Life Planning is a dynamic, backward thinking process to help individuals, couples, families, or family-owned businesses:

- **Define their ideal future vision**
- **Identify the directional strategies required to make that vision reality**
- **Achieve a consistent and meaningful career and life**
- **Drive the achievement of this future vision**

You obviously want to successfully develop and implement a Strategic Career and Life Plan (or else why read this book?). The first step is to get you to think about different important life concepts. To this end, Parts 1 and 2 of this book are designed to help you start thinking and get organized before drafting a plan. They also set up who else will be involved on your planning team and in a parallel process that incorporates key stakeholders you select.

Now, let's take a closer look at the first of the three common-sense premises that were introduced in the preface.

Common-Sense Premise 1: Planning Is Integral to Life

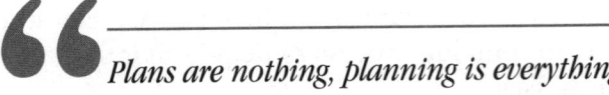
"Plans are nothing, planning is everything."

—Dwight D. Eisenhower

Any person, couple, family, or members of a family-owned business embarking on Strategic Career and Life Planning should first consider this question:

Do you think Strategic Career and Life Planning is:

- ➤ **an event?**
- ➤ **a process?**
- ➤ **a change in your role and career?**
- ➤ **a change in the way you run your day-to-day life?**

The answer is all of the above. Strategic Career and Life Planning is a series of events that form a process. However it is more than that, planning is only useful when it is *planning* for *change*—changes in your role, in your career, and how you run your life day to day.

To gain further understanding of how to proceed from good career and life planning to successful implementation and change, it is valuable to know the five generally accepted functions of management (whether self-management or the management of others).

Functions of Management

1. Planning
2. Organizing
3. Staffing
4. Directing
5. Controlling

As simple as it might seem, most people have forgotten that planning is key to successfully managing both careers and lives. Businesses of all types plan; individuals should also. It is a basic function of life and of self-management.

People seem to have lost sight of the fact that planning is a part of life. It is the first step in the "how to" of a fulfilling career and life. It should lead all the other functions that go into successfully managing your life and career.

A Strategic Career and Life Plan incorporates three overriding goals. They are:

GOAL 1: Develop a strategic career and life plan for your life and career

GOAL 2: Ensure its successful implementation and change

GOAL 3: Continually improve and sustain high performance throughout your life

Common-Sense Premise 2: People Support What They Help Create

> *"The more you are like yourself, the less you are like anyone else. That makes you unique, and helps you be creative."*
>
> —Walt Disney

The first year of Strategic Career and Life Planning involves creating the necessary Strategic Career and Life Plans and documents. In addition to the actual planning undertaken by you, you and your spouse or partner, your family, or the members of your family business, a "parallel process" will be conducted to solicit input and feedback from key stakeholders, which can be anyone with a stake in the success or failure of your plan. In other words, the people close to you and those you trust will be asked to play devil's advocate, coach, mentor, and/or supporter for your plan implementation. You need to solicit their input on each draft document as it is developed, and before it is finalized. This increases the level of support for your plan and strengthens the plan itself.

This strategy is very simple—it means that you should not plan in a vacuum. Instead, involve the people who matter to you as you do your planning. Don't wait until you are finished planning or they will be less likely to support you as you implement the plan. In addition, by involving these key people, you benefit from a host of new and different ideas that will improve your plan. This is because different perspectives can yield a wealth of opportunities and ideas.

The best way to ensure success in involving others is through face-to-face discussions.

The Purpose of Parallel-Process Meetings with Key Stakeholders

- ➤ To explain the planning effort and their importance to it and to you
- ➤ To explain the draft documents
- ➤ To solicit input and comments on the draft

As you develop each phase, share your Strategic Career and Life Plan with:

- ➤ Team members (spouse, partner, family members)
- ➤ Key stakeholders (also may include your spouse or family)

Any planning process that excludes the involvement and ideas of others will have serious problems with successful implementation. Everyone in the world is interdependent on one another in some aspect.

Planning Tip: *Guarantee your key stakeholders that their feedback is valued and will be seriously considered. Input is being gathered from many people, however, and it is unlikely that all of it will appear in the final plan.*

Common-Sense Premise 3: Systems Thinking

> *"Problems that are created by our current level of thinking can't be solved by that same level of thinking."*
>
> —Albert Einstein

Systems Thinking is the framework for all the career and life planning and change that will follow in this book. The Systems Thinking approach is a way to clarify and simplify planning and implementation. It is developed around four phases:

A Output

B Feedback

C Input

D Throughput

Environment (E) is a fifth phase that plays a considerable role as the context for the other four phases. The graphic below illustrates the process you will follow in the book.

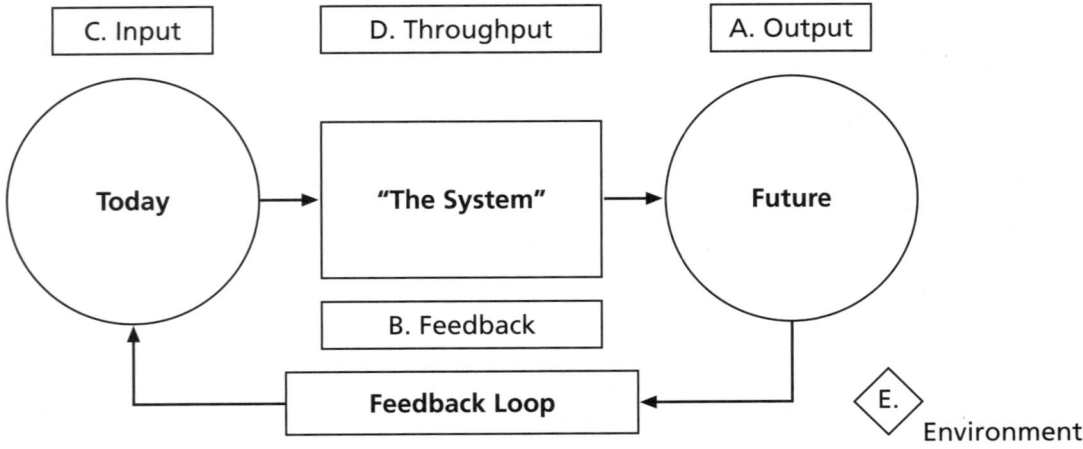

Systems Thinking Approach—
A New Orientation to Life

Systems: _____

"A set of components that work together for the benefit of the whole."

A **Output** refers your ideal future vision and purpose (mission) in your own terms. Output is the realization of your desired future. It asks the question:

"Where do I (we) want to be at X time in the future?"

B **Feedback** or goals are the measures of success in achieving your vision and purpose. By tracking, measuring, and feeding back the status of the results answers the questions:

"How will I (we) know when I get there? What is the measurable scoreboard or feedback for success?"

C **Input** is information to use as your primary means for deciding how to move forward from today. It asks the questions:

"Where am I (we) today? What primary themes or strategies should I adopt to close the gap between Phase C—today—and Phase A—the ideal future?"

These strategies lead you to:

D **Throughput** which consists of a set of specific actions and changes to achieve your desired Output. It answers the immediate question:

"What specific actions will lead me to my desired ideal future vision?"

E **Environment.** As the picture shows, the four-phase circular system is influenced by a wild card, the ever-changing environment. This questions:

"What aspects of the world around me must be considered in the planning process?"

It doesn't matter whether the system is a human body, a copy machine, a car, a couple, a family, or a manufacturing plant. These key elements always act as a framework (or locators and guideposts) for Systems Thinking.

The four key elements illustrated here are the ABCD of Systems Thinking (E plays a role too, but is the context for A through D). They are the four phases of Strategic Career and Life Planning.

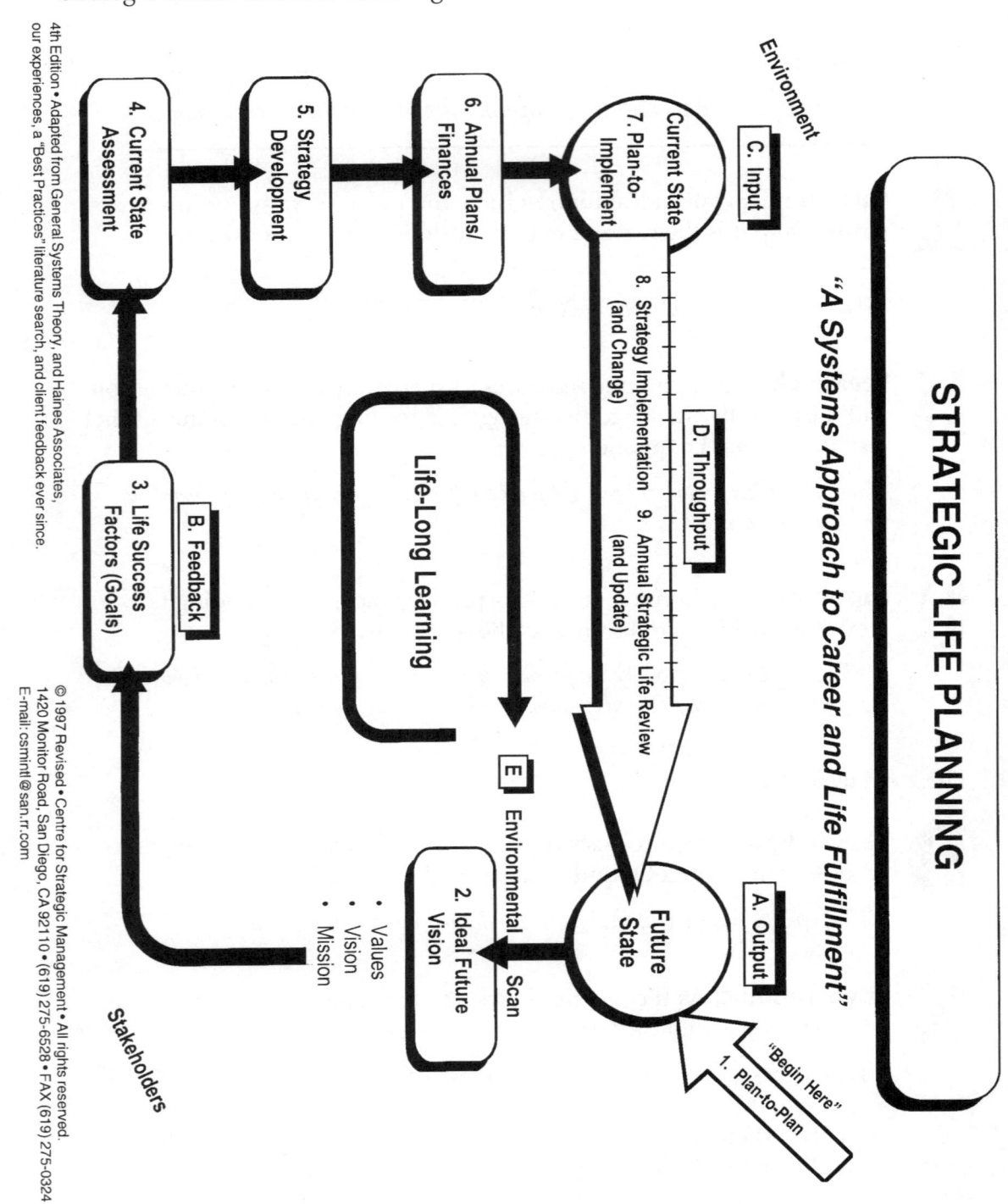

PART 2

Getting Ready to Plan: Setting the Stage

> *"If you don't know where you're going, any road will get you there."*
>
> —Yogi Berra

The Environment: Revolutionary and Global Changes

It is worthwhile to consider E, the environmental aspect of Systems Planning at this stage, as it will influence the ABCDs of your Strategic Career and Life Plan. The world is in an era of revolutionary change. The 1990s saw astonishing changes around the globe, including the reunification of Germany, instantaneous global communication via the Internet, free trade in the European Union, and the strong emergence of the personal computer industry to name a few.

In today's workplace, almost everyone is effected by or involved in some type of fundamental change. The change may be from technology, finances, competition, human resources, materials, and many other potential factors. New and existing industries will appear and grow dramatically in the 21st century. Some possibilities, in addition to the internet, include microelectronics, biotechnology, telecommunications, civil aviation, robotics, and all types of cottage industries. The question then, is what does all this mean to individuals, couples, and families.

Action Task

Take time now to scan the environment around you. Review current environmental trends and consider how, over the next five years, they might influence aspects of society, careers or professions, local or national economics, politics, technology, industry, the competition, business customers, and/or the community.

In the spaces below, looking out over the next three to five years, list three environmental trends—projections, opportunities, threats—that could affect your Strategic Career and Life Plan over its lifetime.

Society

1. _____
2. _____
3. _____

Careers or Professions

1. _____
2. _____
3. _____

Economics

1. _____
2. _____
3. _____

Politics

1. _____
2. _____
3. _____

Technology

1. _____
2. _____
3. _____

Industry

1. _____
2. _____
3. _____

Competition

1. _____
2. _____
3. _____

Business Customers

1. _____
2. _____
3. _____

Community

1. _____
2. _____
3. _____

Career Thinking

In today's world, it is common for most adults to have anywhere from two to four different "careers" rather than one. How many "careers" have you had already?

- ❏ One Full-time Job/Career
- ❏ Two
- ❏ Three

Current Career:

Potential Future Careers:

1. _____
2. _____
3. _____

Planning Tip: *Strategic Career and Life Planning will help guide a career change, ensuring that you are changing careers for good reasons and achieving your objectives in doing so.*

Action Task

Create a 100-item to-do list for your lifetime. In addition to career moves, now is a good time to consider other goals or desires in anticipation of drafting your Strategic Career and Life Plan. Compile a list of 100 things you would like to do in your lifetime. Include things such as learning new skills, having children, participating in an activity, travel, spending time with family, and anything else that comes to mind.

1. _____
2. _____
3. _____
4. _____
5. _____
6. _____
7. _____
8. _____
9. _____
10. _____
11. _____
12. _____
13. _____
14. _____
15. _____
16. _____
17. _____
18. _____
19. _____
20. _____
21. _____
22. _____
23. _____
24. _____
25. _____
26. _____
27. _____
28. _____
29. _____
30. _____
31. _____
32. _____
33. _____
34. _____
35. _____
36. _____
37. _____
38. _____
39. _____
40. _____
41. _____
42. _____
43. _____
44. _____
45. _____
46. _____
47. _____
48. _____
49. _____
50. _____

MORE

MORE

51. _____
52. _____
53. _____
54. _____
55. _____
56. _____
57. _____
58. _____
59. _____
60. _____
61. _____
62. _____
63. _____
64. _____
65. _____
66. _____
67. _____
68. _____
69. _____
70. _____
71. _____
72. _____
73. _____
74. _____
75. _____

76. _____
77. _____
78. _____
79. _____
80. _____
81. _____
82. _____
83. _____
84. _____
85. _____
86. _____
87. _____
88. _____
89. _____
90. _____
91. _____
92. _____
93. _____
94. _____
95. _____
96. _____
97. _____
98. _____
99. _____
100. _____

Anything else?

CRITICAL ISSUES LIST

What are the five to ten most important, biggest, or most critical issues facing you today as an individual? What bothers you or what do you think about when you get up in the morning?

1. _____
2. _____
3. _____
4. _____
5. _____
6. _____
7. _____
8. _____
9. _____
10. _____

Planning Tip: *Keep this list in mind as you proceed through this book. Staying aware of these issues will help ensure that they are addressed as part of your career and life planning.*

Plan-to-Plan:
The Organizing and Tailoring Step

"Plan-to-Plan" is the first step before you do your actual planning. It refers to the need to get educated, get organized, and tailor this process to your needs. It results in a more rational, logical planning sequence. This step is vital to the success of your Career and Life Plan.

The first step in your Strategic Career and Life Planning, is to define your planning team. Determining the size of the planning team will be the first "tough choice" you have to make in the planning process. Individuals and couples may choose to have only themselves on the team, but Strategic Career and Life Planning works best when the right people are involved working on the right (difficult) issues.

When choosing your core planning team members, try to include people who have the following characteristics regarding support for the planning team:

- **A sense of direction where the plan might go**
- **Ownership and commitment to support the plan and its people**
- **A broad perspective on the plan and its future environment**

For example, if you are constructing a plan for a couple, perhaps one or two other key stakeholders such as family members or close friends should join you on the planning team. All the other stakeholders who could be involved would out-number and overwhelm you. Thus, rather than being part of the planning team, these other people are treated separately as "key stakeholders."

Planning Tip: *Any group larger than two-four people usually needs a facilitator to help the group work effectively. You may wish to add a facilitator to your planning team, but this book also serves as the trainer, expert, and process facilitator, freeing you to work in a more independent fashion.*

ACTION TASK

Select the type of team you will work with from the list below.

My Core Planning Team includes myself and:

❏ one other person/my spouse

❏ my family

❏ family business partners

Members of my Core Planning Team:

1. _____
2. _____
3. _____
4. _____
5. _____
6. _____

How far out into the future do I want to plan?

(Typically 1-5 years or until a certain age or event occurs.)

My team will plan backward from this date:

Identify Stakeholders

The next step is to define the key stakeholders who should be involved in your planning, but are not on the planning team. A stakeholder is anyone who has a "stake" in the success or failure of your Strategic Career and Life Plan.

Stakeholders might include your family members, friends, colleagues, supervisors, or religious authority. Keep in mind, "People support what they help create." Your stakeholders might include community members and business associates, as well as clients you serve. As mentioned earlier, stakeholders can be part of your larger planning community or a few could be members of the core planning team that does the hard work of document drafting.

Potential Stakeholders

1. _____
2. _____
3. _____
4. _____
5. _____
6. _____
7. _____
8. _____
9. _____
10. _____

Plan Reviewers

Once you have identified your potential stakeholders, go back to the list and circle at least three key people whom you want to involve in reviewing the planning documents as you develop them. Criteria for selecting reviewers:

> **Those who can provide comments that will improve your plan**

> **Those whose support is critical to the success of your plan**

Keep in mind that involving others in the planning process helps reduce resistance they may have to your desired changes.

Decision-Making by Consensus

The next task is to determine with your planning team members how decisions will be made in this process. The consensus process is recommended. Consensus means making decisions by general agreement. Some guidelines for planning by consensus are provided below.

➤ Take a thoughtful approach, allow as much discussion and decision-making time as each member requires. Operate as a team.

➤ Each member vows to support the group decision, even if it is not exactly the decision the individual wanted.

➤ All sides to an issue are presented and full discussion is promoted, though a time limit—determined by the team—may be imposed.

➤ Focus on the substance of the discussion, the spirit, or intent, not the person.

➤ Know that decisions may be tentative (a draft) and subject to validation/changes after consulting with the key stakeholders.

Potential Barriers

To help you "plan-to-plan," here are some things you should think about in advance. Any of these can become barriers in the Strategic Life and Career Planning process.

1. Failure to believe in success
2. Lack of commitment to the plan
3. Insufficient time and resource allocated to implementing the plan
4. Day-to-day pressures dominate
5. Focus is limited when priorities are not set
6. Unwilling to be visionary, proactive, and creative
7. Tough choices are avoided
8. No system for measuring success
9. History of mistakes or failure in previous attempts at career or life planning
10. Inadequate perseverance for completing the career or life plan
11. SPOTS Syndrome—Strategic Plan on Top Shelf, with no plan for implementation or follow-up
12. Failure of long-term momentum
13. Failure to provide the needed resources (financial and personnel) to implement
14. Conflicting directions/priorities among family members or between a couple
15. Conflicts and poor interpersonal skills among family members or between a couple

Recognizing and Overcoming Barriers

Review the list of potential barriers on the previous page, then list situations or concerns in your own life that might prevent you from being fully ready to draft and implement a Strategic Career and Life Plan. Feel free to draw from the provided list or contribute your own ideas.

My potential barriers:

1. _____
2. _____
3. _____
4. _____
5. _____

Strategies for overcoming barriers:
(For example: delay planning until other things get taken care of, be alert for barriers to ensure they don't occur, etc.)

1. _____
2. _____
3. _____
4. _____
5. _____

Reflecting on your state of mind, body, and spirit can also be a valuable planning step as you prepare for major or minor life changes. The "Balance in Body, Mind, and Spirit" questionnaire which follows will help you assess your areas of strength and areas in which you may want to focus for improvements.

BALANCE IN BODY, MIND, AND SPIRIT

Instruction #1: Please answer each question on a 1-5 scale.

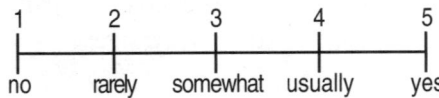

I. Body

_____ 1. Do you have specific ways in which you regularly keep your stress levels under control?

_____ 2. Do you practice a good time management system that includes a priority setting and effectiveness focus; not just efficiencies?

_____ 3. Do you get adequate restful sleep at night?

_____ 4. Do you exercise regularly?

_____ 5. Are you physically fit and "in-shape"?

_____ 6. Is your health good overall?

_____ 7. Do you eat properly and nutritionally?

_____ 8. Do you take adequate lengthy (7+ days) vacations each year?

_____ 9. Do you take adequate short breaks in your work life?

_____ 10. Do you have trust and confidence in yourself to handle stress, emergencies, and crises well?

[ ] *Subtotal for "Body"*

II. Mind

_____ 11. Do you have and live a clear and personal purpose statement for your life?

_____ 12. Do you have and follow a Strategic Life Plan for yourself with clear goals and objectives?

_____ 13. Do you take quiet time regularly for yourself to meditate, relax deeply, and clear your thoughts and stress?

_____ 14. Are you constantly learning and growing?

_____ 15. Do you have and pursue clear career goals?

_____ 16. Do you have and pursue educational goals for yourself?

_____ 17. Do you have adequate private time for yourself?

_____ 18. Do you have and pursue hobbies and avocations outside of work?

_____ 19. Are you a strategic, conceptual, and systems thinker?

_____ 20. Do you act with conscious intent?

[ ] *Subtotal for "Mind"*

BALANCE IN BODY, MIND AND SPIRIT

III. Spirit

_____ 21. Do you have and live a clear set of personal beliefs, values and/or philosophies?

_____ 22. Is there a clear spiritual or religious component to your life?

_____ 23. Are you rarely "out of control" emotionally and/or rarely have emotional outbursts?

_____ 24. Do you have a positive or upbeat personality?

_____ 25. Do you have a strong sense of self-worth and self-esteem?

_____ 26. Do you rarely allow others to negatively impact your dignity and respect as a human being without stopping them?

_____ 27. Do you recognize and take time to celebrate your life's successes regularly?

_____ 28. Are you in love with someone?

_____ 29. Do you spend adequate time enjoying the beauty of nature?

_____ 30. Do you have beauty around you in your daily life?

[ ] *Subtotal for "Spirit"*

[ ] Total Score

Determining Average Score	Note:
_____ Body/10 = Average = _____	Maximum possible total score = 150 points.
_____ Mind/10 = Average = _____	An average total score = 90 points.
_____ Spirit/10 = Average = _____	
_____ Total/30 = Average = _____	

Instruction #2:

List your top 3-5 areas of excellence	List your top 3-5 areas needing most improvement
1.	1.
2.	2.
3.	3.
4.	4.
5.	5.

Successful Career and Life Planning

PART 3

The ABC Phases

> *" You can and should shape your own future; because, if you don't, somebody else surely will!"*
>
> —J. Barker

> *" We need to learn how to spend our time and effort working on the future, instead of continually rearranging the past."*
>
> —Philip Crosby

30

Phase A: Output—
Creating Your Ideal Future

*The only limits, as always, are those of vision."*

–James Broughton

Your ideal future vision is the place to begin your Strategic Career and Life Planning. This step is concerned with formulating dreams that are worth believing in and fighting for. At this stage in the Strategic Career and Life Planning process, the fear that "it can't be done!" is irrelevant. Turning the vision into reality is part of the backward thinking process that will be pursued after the vision is created. For now, the sky's the limit!

Three challenges are issued during this step:

CHALLENGE 1: To articulate core values for the future that will guide day-to-day behavior.

CHALLENGE 2: To conduct a visioning process in order to develop a Vision Statement of your dreams, hopes, and desired image of your future.

CHALLENGE 3: To develop a Mission Statement for the future describing why you as individuals, couples, or families exist.

CHALLENGE 1 Core Values

Core personal values guide day-to-day behaviors. Sometimes they are called beliefs and philosophies. Core personal values are few in number.

CORE PERSONAL VALUES

Rank the following ideas and activities in order of importance to you personally at the present time. Place any number between 1 and 15 in the Actual column. 1 = Very Important, 15 = Not at All Important, in your current situation.

Next, go through the exercise again, this time using the Desired column to reflect how you wish these ideas and activities were ordered in your life. Again, 1 = Very important, 15 = Not at All Important, to your desired future.

Core Personal Values	Actual	Desired
1. Good relationships with colleagues/family		
2. Professional reputation/respect		
3. Achievement of organization/family goals		
4. Teamwork and collaboration		
5. Leisure time for enjoyment/fun		
6. Wealth and prosperity		
7. Fitness and health		
8. Contribution/service to society/community		
9. Acknowledging/recognizing other's achievements		
10. Autonomy/freedom to act		
11. Personal growth		
12. Time with family/close friends		
13. Ethical behaviors		
14. Excitement and challenge		
15. Spiritual/religious time		

Once you have finished both columns of the exercise, share and compare your answers with your planning team or with key stakeholders.

DEFINING CORE PERSONAL VALUES

List your core personal values and the key statements that define them so that these can serve as concrete guides to your preferred or desired behaviors.

The goal of this challenge is to clarify which personal values are most important to you. To accomplish this, look back over the list of personal values and choose between 3 and 5 that you value most highly or that you wish to give greater attention to in your life. Then, develop a series of bullet statements about each core personal value in order to fully define and share them in a useful way.

Core Personal Value: _____

-
-
-

Core Personal Value: _____

-
-
-

Core Personal Value: _____

-
-
-

Core Personal Value: _____

-
-
-

Core Personal Value: _____

-
-
-

Action Task

Once you have defined your core personal values, you may want to do a quick current-state assessment of how you are doing in terms of living these values today. Answer the following questions:

1. Which of my core personal values am I best at today?

- _____
- _____
- _____

2. Which of my core personal values are most in need of improvement right now? (Tip: Ask your key stakeholders these questions also. See if they agree.)

- _____
- _____
- _____

3. What behaviors will you change or modify in order to improve your ability to "walk the talk" of your core personal values?

                                                                 By When?

1. _____
2. _____
3. _____
4. _____
5. _____

> *Remember, character does matter. Never forget that character is what you are when no one is looking."*
>
> –J. C. Watts

CHALLENGE 2 Vision Statement

In order to develop a vision for the future, you may first have to examine the boundaries that you have placed on yourself. Boundaries limit your current thinking. For the best visioning, identify current personal boundaries to your thinking and let go of them for the next hour.

CURRENT BOUNDARIES

Complete the vision tasks below. Some examples of possible "current boundaries" or limitations are listed to the left. In the right column, describe any that relate to your life.

Example of Current Boundaries	My Current Boundaries
1. My job	
2. My customers	
3. My personal values	
4. My skills and capabilities	
5. My uniqueness, distinctive characteristics	
6. My geographic location	
7. My history, environment, family background	
8. My race, ethnicity	
9. My current level of leadership, excellence, service, quality, etc.	
10. What I am known for; my reputation or image	
11. My educational background	
12. My friends, relatives, family relationships	
13. My church, community service	
14. My profession	
15. My hobbies	

Action Task

Review the time frame you selected for your Strategic Career and Life Plan in Part 2, then find a relaxed place to sit, put down your pen, and focus on the exercise below.

Your Personal Ideal Future Vision

Spend 10 minutes focusing on your personal ideal future. Envision what the future will be like at the end of the time frame you have established. Your imagination should place no boundaries on this vision. Focus on desires and concepts, not on specifics. Perfectionism and boundaries limit your ability to create your ideal.

Be creative. Be innovative. Be limitless. Go for your ideal!

Next, write your thoughts here as a stream of consciousness—do not stop to worry about sentence structure, spelling, or proper grammar.

_____
_____
_____
_____
_____
_____
_____
_____
_____
_____
_____
_____
_____
_____

LIFE ROLES: PERSONAL IDEAL FUTURE VISION

Expand your Personal Ideal Future Vision for each of your life roles, as outlined on the next few pages.

1. Personal

Physical Fitness: _____

Health: _____

Mental: _____

Learning: _____

Emotional: _____

Spiritual: _____

2. Interpersonal

Social/Friends: _____

Sense of Community: _____

Service to Others: _____

Home: _____

Spouse: _____

Immediate family/Children/Siblings: _____

_____

Extended Family (parents, grandparents, cousins): _____

_____

MORE

MORE

3. Career

Careers/Industry/Roles: _____

Work Relationships (Supervisors/Subordinates/Peers): _____
_____

Quality of Work Life: _____

Organizational Culture/Values: _____

Partnerships (Customers/Systems/Alliances): _____
_____

Education/Degrees: _____

4. Wealth

Wealth/Accumulation: _____

Wealth/Distribution: _____

5. Lifestyle

Lifestyle balance: _____

Experiences/Travel: _____

Character/Reputation: _____

Avocation/Hobbies: _____

Celebrations: _____

Environment/Earth: _____

Action Task

Vision Statement Draft 1: Personal Vision

Use the ideas and goals in the previous exercise task to develop a short, positive, and inspiring vision statement. This will be the first draft of your final vision statement.

My Vision of an Ideal Future is:

_____
_____
_____
_____
_____
_____

Vision Statement Draft 2: Consensus Vision

Share Draft 1 with your entire planning team. You may also share it with your key stakeholders in a parallel process. Using the feedback and ideas from these discussions, as a team, develop a draft #2 Consensus Vision.

Our Ideal Future Vision at Year _____ is:

_____
_____
_____
_____
_____
_____

Note: The appendix contains an example of a vision statement.

CHALLENGE 3 Mission Statement

A mission statement tends to be more realistic than a vision statement and answers three key questions: Who? what? and why? The following Mission Development Triangle illustrates the steps for developing a mission statement.

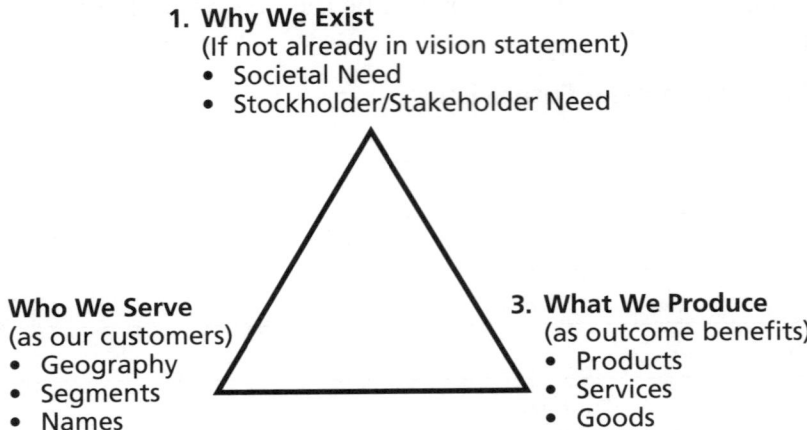

For example:

Who—We all serve others in addition to ourselves. "Who" may include your family, your work colleagues, etc.

What—We all deliver some kind of results or outputs from the use of our talents. These might include writing books, teaching sports, community service, playing music, or the results defined by your profession.

CREATING A MISSION

Each individual should complete the mission development exercise by answering the questions below. Answer the questions quickly. Don't worry about using the perfect words; just get your key concepts down on paper.

Questions you may want to ask yourself about your life's mission include:

1. What are my unique gifts and talents?

2. How do I want to use these unique gifts and talents?

3. How do I specifically contribute to society? Who do I serve?

4. What do I want for myself?

5. What makes me feel good about myself?

6. How do I make a difference in this world?

7. Be selfish for a minute: What do I really, really want?

8. Which of the roles in my vision are most important to me? Why?

9. What do I want my epitaph to say?

Action Task

Once you have developed your mission ideas, meet with your planning team and key stakeholders and come to an agreement on these three key questions from the Mission Development Triangle: Why do I (we) exist? Who do I (we) serve? What do I (we) produce?

Mission Development Triangle:

Why do I/we exist?

Who do I/we serve?

What do I/we produce?

REFINED MISSION STATEMENT

A refined mission statement should be:

- ➤ Realistic and feasible
- ➤ Understandable
- ➤ Concise
- ➤ Broad and continuing in nature, but not so broad as to be meaningless
- ➤ Stated in terms of output (results) rather than activities (inputs or throughputs)
- ➤ Use specific and purposeful words, especially the names of your customers (who you serve), your products, services, and talents

Using the information developed on the previous page and the Mission Development Triangle, write your mission statement below.

For example:

"Our mission is to serve (ourselves and others) with the (products and services) in order to achieve (why we exist)."

My/Our Mission is:

_____
_____
_____
_____
_____
_____
_____
_____
_____
_____

Note: *The appendix contains a sample mission statement.*

Phase B: Feedback—Measuring Success

Goals are the "quantifiable measurements of success" in achieving your vision, mission, and core values on a year-by-year basis.

(Note: goals are often called Key Success Factors, or KSFs, for the purposes of this document, we will use the simpler term "goals.")

Setting goals is a necessary step for Strategic Career and Life Planning and encourages concrete answers to three critical questions during plan implementation:

- **How do you know when you are successful?**
- **How do you know when you're getting into trouble?**
- **If off course, what corrective actions should you take?**

When developing your goals, you first need to define the areas that will be measured. At a minimum, there are three specific areas to be measured and tracked.

- **"Customer" satisfaction (serving others)**
- **Financial results**
- **Personal/couple satisfaction**

GOAL SETTING

Make a list of general goals that represent what you need in order to achieve your vision within the established three- to five-year time frame (planning horizon). Your different life roles are a good place to begin.

1. _____
2. _____
3. _____
4. _____
5. _____
6. _____
7. _____
8. _____
9. _____
10. _____

Making Goals Measurable

Once goals are defined, specific measurements and yearly targets can be set. Ten is the preferred maximum number of goals—limiting the number forces a focus on what is key to success.

Goals should be set with specific measures such as:

QUALITY as perceived by those you serve, i.e., the quality of your work or leisure activities such as sports and hobbies.

QUANTITY such as how many times a week you plan to exercise. Ratios may also be used, such as saving a percentage of your income every month.

TIME such as a date by which you will complete a key task.

COST such as the dollars in the family budget or the percentage you plan to tithe to the church

Now that you have a picture of what is important to measure, it's time to build a complete set of goals for tracking plan achievement. These goals should be ones you can evaluate objectively to know whether they have been achieved.

> ***Planning Tip:*** *Focus on the vital outputs, not the trivial activities. The operative word is key, not comprehensive, goals.*

Note: *The appendix contains examples of measurable goals.*

Action Task

For each goal, you need to set a target or measure of success for the final year in your three- to five-year planning horizon. This should be a realistic target that you are deeply committed to achieving.

Using the form below, list your top 10 or fewer goals in the left-hand column. Establish the year by which you want to achieve the goal and record that in the right-hand column. In the middle column, note your current status for each goal. Be clear where you stand on each of these goals right now—have you started, are you halfway to achieving, do you need to take some initial steps or acquire some resources before you can begin?

Note: *Often, data on your current status will be missing or does not exist except for financial measures. This is normal. Success in the first year is often just two tasks: (1) determining the goal and its measurement, and (2) setting in place the way to measure.*

Goals (with measures)	Current Status	Target Date
1.		
2.		
3.		
4.		
5.		
6.		
7.		
8.		
9.		
10.		

Planning Tip: *When completed, this chart becomes a report card of success similar to the report cards you receive in school. You should check it quarterly to see whether you are close to achieving these goal targets.*

Yearly Reporting

Lastly, you need to establish a system for measuring, tracking, and reporting on these goals. The system is similar to methods used to track household budgets and checking accounts. You may want to use the Yearly Reporting Format on the next page. There is also an example in the appendix.

1. You are responsible for developing, tracking, and reporting on your success in achieving your goals.

2. Use the goals and timelines you set on previous pages to fill in the following three columns:

    ➤ Goals (with measures)

    ➤ Baseline Year (current status of goal)

    ➤ Target Goal Year (the year by which you plan to have this goal achieved)

3. On the next page, fill in the "intermediate target" (or measures) on a year-by-year basis so you can track "actual" progress.

Planning Tip: *Goals are easy to describe and discuss. However, they are often difficult to develop without time for reflection and revision. Keep working on your goals and fine-tune them over time.*

YEARLY REPORTING FORMAT (TARGET VS. ACTUAL)

Plan Coordinator: (you) _____

Goals	Baseline Year (current)	Intermediate Targets							Target Goal Year
		Year 1		Year 2		Year 3		Year 4		
		Target	Actual	Target	Actual	Target	Actual	Target	Actual	Target	Actual
1.											
2.											
3.											
4.											
5.											
6.											
7.											
8.											
9.											
10.											

Note: Each Goal might be tracked at different quarters (target vs. actual) depending on when the measurement is taken. However, each Goal needs to be measured and reported at least yearly. A quarterly chart like this can also be developed to look at all Goals each quarter.

49

Phase C: Input—Developing and Converting Strategies into Action

> *"People are successful, not because of the hundred and one good little actions they take to save money on paper clips and telephone calls, but because of one or two major strategies that are brilliant!"*
>
> —Adapted from Dr. Michael J. Kami

Phase C of the Strategic Career and Life Planning model takes stock of current conditions. Core strategies are then established to close the gap between your future vision and today. These core strategies become the organizing framework to guide the rest of the planning process—from the strategic to the annual action plans and follow-up progress reports.

Current state assessment is the first step in Phase C. Honesty is the operative concept here.

The SWOT Approach

SWOT is an acronym for looking at internal—Strengths and Weaknesses—and external—Opportunities and Threats—issues. A SWOT analysis will help pinpoint the gaps between your current situation and your future vision. It also helps suggest appropriate strategies and actions.

Four surveys are provided on the following pages to help you prepare for your SWOT analysis. Your discoveries will be integrated into a full SWOT analysis.

The four surveys are:

- **Personal Skills and Competencies**
- **Career Self Development**
- **Working With Others**
- **Core Competencies**

PERSONAL SKILLS AND COMPETENCIES

Carefully read the list of foundational skills and competencies and rate your abilities in each area on a 1-10 scale, with 1 representing low ability and 10 representing high ability. You may want to make some notes about why you rate yourself as you do.

	Your Score	**Explanation/Notes**
Foundation Skills		
Basic Skill Development		
Thinking Skills		
Personal Qualities		
Competencies		
Resources		
Interpersonal Skills		
Information Handling Skills		
Systems		
Technology		

CAREER SELF-DEVELOPMENT

Complete the assessment below to determine what activities you may want to engage in to better help you in your professional growth.

Yes　No　　　Development Activities　　　　　　　　　　　Comments

❏　❏　I regularly use a resource library or the Internet to check out books, reference materials, and other information.

❏　❏　I buy and read books.

❏　❏　I subscribe to newspapers, newsletters, magazines, and/or executive book summaries.

❏　❏　I belong to and attend professional associations.

❏　❏　I engage in networking activities such as bag lunches, after-work meetings, breakfast meetings, or mentor systems.

❏　❏　I undergo personal skills and personality assessments.

❏　❏　I hold periodic review meetings with key stakeholders/family members.

❏　❏　I attended trade shows or other events within the past year.

What other activities contribute to my career development?

My conclusions

　Areas of Strength:

　Areas of Weakness:

WORKING WITH OTHERS

Which of these are you good at? Assess how often you do the following.

---
1 = Seldom or never   2 = Sometimes   3 = Frequently

_____ 1. I focus on the need of others.

_____ 2. I provide options rather than orders for others to follow.

_____ 3. I try to model openness and provide disclosure to build intimacy.

_____ 4. I let people know what to expect so there are no surprises.

_____ 5. I "talk their talk."

_____ 6. I truly care for people and build personal relationships via acceptance, genuineness, and empathy.

_____ 7. I use thank-you cards to recognize co-workers and staff and to provide positive reinforcement.

_____ 8. I educate my staff by setting an example and providing comprehensive information.

_____ 9. I appreciate the individuality of my support staff.

_____ 10. I try to tap the dreams, visions, and values held by my support staff.

_____ Total (Possible 30 points)

Circle any of the items above that you wish to focus on improving in order to work better with others.

CORE COMPETENCIES

Core competencies are the vital elements that an individual, team, or organization uses to create a competitive edge. Core competencies flow from your unique talents and gifts. Examples might include the ability to teach or to lead, or special skill such as writing computer programs

1. **What are your core current competencies?** List them here, and then add them to your SWOT (strengths) in the analysis activity that follows.

    - _____
    - _____
    - _____

2. **How does the current status of your core competencies compare to the level you would wish to achieve for these same competencies?**

    - _____
    - _____
    - _____

3. **Where is the gap?** List them here, and then add them to your SWOT (weaknesses) in the analysis activity that follows.

    - _____
    - _____
    - _____

SWOT Framework

Now, conduct the SWOT analysis using the information you have discovered in the three assessments you just completed. Summarize the key points here as appropriate, taking time to reflect as you do this.

Step 1: Complete the left side of the chart.

Step 2: Review the strengths you have documented here with your planning team and/or key stakeholders. Make additions and corrections as necessary. (You may find that some issues have two sides in that they are both a strength and a weakness.)

Step 3: Complete the "Suggested Action" column. You should be able to name at least one action to move you toward your vision for each item you listed in the left column. It is not necessary to agree on all these actions. They are starting points to be used as brainstorming tools for the next step developing core strategies, actions, and priorities.

Internal Analysis

Strengths to Build On	Suggested Action
1.	
2.	
3.	
4.	
5.	
6.	
7.	
8.	
9.	

MORE

MORE

Internal Analysis

Weaknesses to Eliminate or Reduce	Suggested Action
1.	
2.	
3.	
4.	
5.	
6.	
7.	
8.	
9.	

External Analysis

Opportunities to Exploit	Suggested Action
1.	
2.	
3.	
4.	
5.	
6.	
7.	
8.	
9.	

MORE

External Analysis

Threats to Ease or Lower	Suggested Action
1.	
2.	
3.	
4.	
5.	
6.	
7.	
8.	
9.	

*The greatest of faults...is to be conscious of none."*

—Thomas Carlyle

Strategy Development

> *"When one door of happiness closes, another opens, but often we look so long at the closed door that we do not see the one which has been opened for us."*
>
> —Helen Keller

Strategy development creates the core strategies to bridge gaps between your ideal future vision and your current state assessment. Here's something to keep in mind as you complete the following section: If you always do what you've always done, you'll always get what you've always gotten.

The strategy-development step should result in a focus on three to six core strategies to be implemented by your planning team. Developing a focused set of strategies is a primary means to achieving your ideal future vision and the goals you have previously set as measurable actions. In other words, your goals are your outcomes/results/ends and strategies are the primary means. These strategies become the "glue" or the organizing principles and priorities that serve as a framework to set annual action plans. Keep in mind that these strategies should apply to the entire period and individual, couple, family, or business unit for which you are planning. Thus, they may not be applicable to each person or business partner.

CORE STRATEGIES

What do you believe are the three to six core strategies you should pursue over the life of your planning horizon to achieve your ideal future vision and the goals you've already set? Based on your vision and goals, you probably will have a mix of personal and professional strategies.

You must be clear as to what results you desire. If you did your planning process thoroughly up to this point, this list should be simple to develop. You have probably been informally discussing possible strategies throughout this planning process as you developed earlier documents.

The fewer the number of core strategies, the better. Making tough choices here in order to "focus, focus, focus" is the key to success in almost all Successful Career and Life Planning. Be sure these core strategies are written in the active tense, with an action verb and a complete sentence. The Appendix contains some examples.

1. _____
   _____

2. _____
   _____

3. _____
   _____

4. _____
   _____

5. _____
   _____

6. _____
   _____

Next: *Thoroughly rework and refine this list with all planning team members and/or key stakeholders to ensure a consensus on your core strategies.*

Action Task

Develop five to 10 actions to be accomplished over the planning horizon to achieve each core strategy listed on previous page. These are the major activities, personal priorities, and specific changes required over time. When you're done, go back and place an asterisk (*) next to up to four priorities to be completed over the next 12 months.

Core Strategy 1

Action items over the planning horizon	Who	Deadline
1.		
2.		
3.		
4.		
5.		
6.		
7.		
8.		
9.		
10.		

* = Next year's top priorities

Core Strategy 2

Action items over the planning horizon	Who	Deadline
1.		
2.		
3.		
4.		
5.		
6.		
7.		
8.		
9.		
10.		

* = Next year's top priorities

Core Strategy 3

Action items over the planning horizon	Who	Deadline
1.		
2.		
3.		
4.		
5.		
6.		
7.		
8.		
9.		
10.		

* = Next year's top priorities

MORE

MORE

Core Strategy 4

Action items over the planning horizon	Who	Deadline
1.		
2.		
3.		
4.		
5.		
6.		
7.		
8.		
9.		
10.		

* = Next year's top priorities

Core Strategy 5

Action items over the planning horizon	Who	Deadline
1.		
2.		
3.		
4.		
5.		
6.		
7.		
8.		
9.		
10.		

* = Next year's top priorities

Personal Annual Work Plan

Now it is time to "cascade" your Strategic Career and Life Plan down to annual plans, priorities, finances, and, eventually, to individual yearly reviews. This is where the rubber meets the road. The idea that "excellence is a matter of doing 10,000 things right" is key to any successful implementation.

In this process, you will develop a plan of specific tasks you need to accomplish over the next 12 months. You also will prioritize your tasks for the year and then name the resources/responsibilities required to implement them.

Reflect

Use the strategy and action items work done earlier as a guide. Your task is to interpret for yourself how all the planning work done previously applies to you personally.

Write

Each member of a couple, family, or family-owned business who is involved in this planning should fill out the Personal Annual Plan form that follows, listing the specific tasks needed to accomplish each core strategy. Make a photocopy of the form so that each of you will have a worksheet for developing your Annual Work Plans.

Review

It is not enough to have each person develop an annual work plan in isolation from others on the planning team. What is needed is an annual review meeting of all planning team members. At this meeting, all annual work plans are shared, critiqued, and refined based on their relevance to the top priorities for each core strategy.

Organizing each person's work plan under the same core strategies is the key to an integrated and thorough implementation. This cannot be stressed enough. By organizing everyone's annual work plans under the same core strategies you will begin to think about achieving strategies rather than thinking about only yourself or turf battles and turf protection.

The Personal Annual Work Plan

Use the Personal Annual Work Plan format that follows to document your plans.

- **Do a separate work plan page for each core strategy, i.e., six strategies equals six pages.**

- **List the tasks you will do in the next year under the Actions column. Relate it back to the annual priority actions defined earlier by listing the number the task relates to in the left column (yearly priority number).**

- **Fill in the next four columns regarding**

    —what support/resources are needed

    —who is responsible for the task

    —who else should be involved in the task

    —when it will be done

- **The Status column is to be used during the year to list accomplishments and share them throughout the year on a quarterly basis (more on this later).**

PERSONAL ANNUAL "WORK PLAN" FORMAT   Date: _____

#1 Strategies: _____

Yearly Priority #	Actions	Support/Resources Needed	Who Responsible?	Who Else to Involve?	When Done?	Status During Year

65

Resource Allocation Plan

Once you have completed your annual action plans, it is time to review whether you need to change the way you spend your financial resources. Good budgeting needs to follow annual work planning. This will enable you to achieve a more focused allocation of your money based on your Strategic Career and Life Plan.

It is possible there will be some conflict between current allocations vs. future action priorities. This is normal and desired as it will help you focus your time and energy toward achieving your Strategic Career and Life Plan rather than spending your resources in ways that may not advance your goals. It is important to build a budget that focuses on your top priorities, hence, the importance of the column called "Support/Resources Needed" on the Annual Plan Form. Be sure to fill in the Support/Resources column on the Annual Work Plan Form.

A Resource Allocation Plan form for determining personal expenses is provided on the next page. Make a photocopy of the form and use it over and over. Creating and managing a budget is as crucial for individuals, couples, and families as it is for a business. Don't leave your ability to fund your desires to chance. If this changes the way you spend your money and your personal time, that is the whole point of this process.

> **Note:** *Budgeting is usually a complex process for a business and is out of the scope of the book. Many software programs are available to help you through the process.*

RESOURCE ALLOCATION PLAN FORM

Based on your forecasted monthly income, conduct a Resource Allocation Plan using this form. Add and delete future resources based on your core strategies. Add items 1 through 18 then subtract the total from your gross monthly income.

Monthly Home Financial Management

Income/Expenses	Actual	Planned
Gross Monthly Income:		
Monthly Expenses:		
1. Home mortgage/rent		
2. Taxes/insurance		
3. Utilities (all)		
4. Food		
—at home		
—outside home		
5. Childcare		
6. Entertainment		
7. Automobile (all expenses)		
8. Life/health/dental insurance/expenses		
9. TV/cable/newspapers/books		
10. Household/yard maintenance		
11. Dry cleaning/laundry		
12. Clothing		
13. Hair care		
14. Travel/vacation		
15. Credit card payments		
16. Memberships/clubs		
17. Savings/Investments		
18. Miscellaneous		
Total Monthly Expenses:		
Net Monthly Excess/Deficit:		

PART 4

Implementing Plans Successfully

> *If you make a commitment to a given field of endeavor, and if you spend the next five years of your life with the magnificent obsession to learn all there is about that field, you can be certain to become a success in that field."*
>
> **–Earl Nightingale**

70

Phase D: Throughput—
Plan to Implement

This phase is the beginning of successful implementation of your Strategic Career and Life Plan leading to a fulfilling career and life.

Plan to Implement

Phase D begins with two primary tasks. The first task is to become "educated" on the issue of change. The second task is to complete a set of plan-to-implement organizing and tailoring tasks very much like the earlier Plan-to-Plan work. The main difference between these similar "Plan-to" steps is that this one deals with that difficult subject—change.

This step is the crucial bridge between Strategic Career and Life Planning and implementing that plan successfully and profitably.

The first thing to appreciate is how a person experiences change. The Rollercoaster of Change[SM] that follows provides a diagram of the basic psychology of individual and organizational change.

> *The marvelous richness of human experience would lose something of rewarding joy if there were no limitations to overcome. The hilltop hour would not be half so wonderful if there were no dark valleys to traverse.*"
>
> —Helen Keller

Rollercoaster of Change℠

Study this model and its four basic steps. Each person goes through these steps at their own pace and depth. People often ride several different rollercoasters at the same time (personal, professional, social, and spiritual).

The "hang-in" point is often where success or failure is decided. It is important to "persevere" when times get tough. Once you have studied this basic model, it may be helpful to know that there are sets of major questions that can help you handle change more effectively.

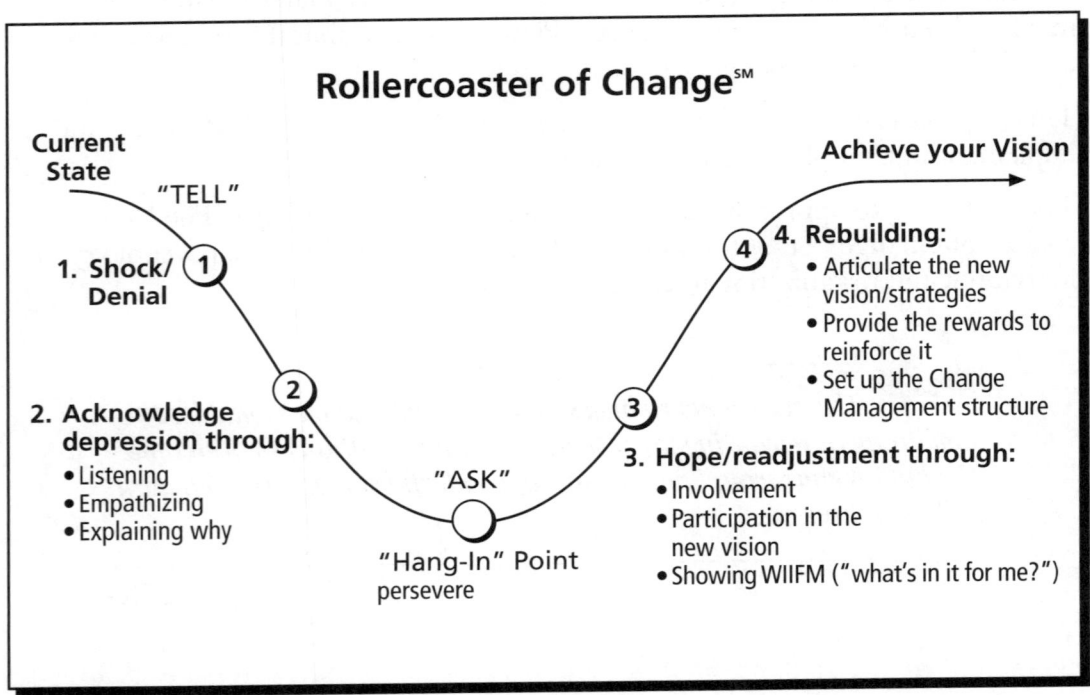

PUTTING CHANGE IN PERSPECTIVE

Make a list of key changes you need to make to guide your implementation. As you prepare to implement these changes, discuss the following questions with your planning team members and/or your key stakeholders.

1. _____
2. _____
3. _____
4. _____
5. _____
6. _____
7. _____
8. _____
9. _____
10. _____

Questions That Help Put Change in Perspective:

1. Not "if," but "when" will I (we) start to go through shock/depression?
2. How deep is the trough? Is it different for each person? What are the implications?
3. How long will it take? Does everyone reach the same stage at the same time?
4. How do I manage change proactively?
5. What new skills do I need to accomplish this?
6. How many different roller coasters will I experience in this change?
7. Are there other changes/roller coasters occurring at the same time?
8. Will I hang in and persevere at the bottom? How?
9. How will I deal with normal resistance in myself and others?
10. How will I create a critical mass to support and achieve my desired change?

Action Task

Review and finalize your Strategic Career and Life Plan now. Package it into a formal document. This document is finalized by using the Keep It Simple Sam/Sarah (KISS) method). This allows the Strategic Career and Life Plan document to be used in a practical day-to-day fashion vs. the dreaded SPOTS Syndrome (Strategic Plan On the Top Shelf—collecting dust).

Use the prototype Strategic Career and Life Planning Final Document which follows as a guide and template.

Note: *The appendix contains an example of a complete Strategic Career and Life Plan.*

Strategic Career and Life Planning Final Document

(Remember: Keep It Simple—12-20 pages maximum)

Sections/Documents	Number of Pages
Introduction	
Cover sheet	2-4
Table of Contents	
Environmental Scanning and Strategic Issues List (optional)	1-2
Ideal Future Vision and Strategies	
Vision (Back-up Details—Optional)	1-2
Mission (Back-up Details—Optional)	1
Personal Values (Bullets—Optional)	1-3
Goals 2-3	
Core Strategies	2-3
—With Action Items/top three priorities for each for next year	
Next Year	
Implementation Plan, including:	2-3
—Change Steering Committee	
—Change and Transition Process/Yearly Comprehensive Map	

Some Final Thoughts on Change

In order to achieve your desired changes, each participant in the Strategic Career and Life Planning process must understand and act on some additional change management concepts. These concepts have to do with nurturing, protecting, encouraging, and rewarding yourself and your plan as time goes on.

> *Let him who would move the world first move himself."*
>
> —**Socrates**

> *You have to be able to manage yourself to succeed, and to set a good example for those who work and live for you. Intelligence, education, and drive are prime requisites for achievement. But they're worthless without the discipline that enables you to transport your abilities to the marketplace. A true achiever is an individual who has reached his or her full potential as a human being."*
>
> —**Raymond C. Johnson**, *The Achievers*

To learn more about how you can manage change and draw support from others review the suggestions that follow.

How Do I Change?

What I Can Do	How Others Can Help
Visualize the new identity you'd like to have.	Advocate change.
Have strong passion for the new identity.	Build a critical mass of informal support.
Develop self-awareness of the change and time to reflect on it.	Get valid feedback from others.
Have faith that I can make the change.	Become involved in some aspect of the change.
Allow yourself to feel anxious.	Give continued positive reinforcement, support, and reassurance.
Practice and practice with the new attitudes and behaviors.	Provide guidance and mentoring.
Become a compassionate self-observer (supportive and enthusiastic about one's self)	Respect the values and dignity of the person implementing change.
Have a sense of humor about the change.	Provide rewards/reinforcement.
Provide self-rewards for the new identity.	Accept the person "as is."
Persistence, persistence, persistence.	Provide education and awareness training on change.

Feedback is the "breakfast of champions." Do you seek it from individuals and collectively to ensure focus on desired outcomes, even when painful? Encourage feedback about yourself from others.

" To be the best, you have to be totally honest with yourself…and others."

—Thurman Thomas

Action Plan for Reinforcing Change

Complete this exercise to develop an action plan for reinforcing change based on all you have learned and considered so far. Your changes are the strategies/actions/tasks in your Strategic Career and Life Plan. This will help you to clarify your own process or journey for changing your own behaviors.

What can I do?	Who should be involved?	Deadline?
1.		
2.		
3.		
4.		

Two Keys to Success

In addition the plans and processes described in this book up to this point, it is helpful to set up a game plan to manage the processes over the life of the planning horizon. A Change Steering Committee is absolutely essential in successfully implementing your Strategic Career and Life Plan and a Yearly Comprehensive Map lists all of the needed implementation processes for the first year of your game plan. A steering committee and a map will help you to manage change so that it won't manage you.

Key 1: Change Steering Committee

To combat the failure to follow "good intention" problems with change, it is helpful to set up a Change Steering Committee to guide, reinforce, and follow-up on the changes indicated by your Strategic Career and Life Plan.

Purpose:

1. To guide and control the implementation of a Strategic Career and Life Plan.

2. To coordinate other major performance improvement projects happening simultaneously alongside the implementation of your Strategic Career and Life Plan.

The steering committee is very similar to the planning team. It can have the same membership as the planning team (usually an individual, couple, family, and/or stakeholders). The committee should meet every one-to-three months depending on the intensity of your implementation schedule. You can elect to follow a parallel process with key stakeholders as needed. These Steering Committee meetings are typically one-half day in length.

Three mandatory agenda items for each of these meetings are:

1. Scan the changing environment for life and career implications.
2. Track your goals and problem-solve issues related to them.
3. Problem-solve issues surrounding the core strategies and top priority actions.

The frequency and intensity of meetings should be less than you put into the planning effort, however. The greater part of your energies should be in implementation rather than meetings. The faster you want implementation to proceed, the more frequently your steering committee should meet.

Propel the implementation of your Strategic Career and Life Plan throughout the year with regular Steering Committee meetings and follow up. Disciplined persistence throughout the year is key. You will "fall off the bike" of implementation during the year. That is normal and to be expected. Just get back on with help from your steering committee.

Define your steering committee parameters below.

ACTION TASK

1. Committee Purpose:

2. Committee Members:

3. Meeting Frequency/Length:

4. Meeting Location:

5. Key Stakeholders:

6. Ways to include them:

Planning Tip: *It is crucial for steering committee meetings to be held on a regular basis in order to pull back from the day-to-day activities, scan status of the Life Plan, and review its implementation as necessary.*

Key 2: Yearly Comprehensive Map

Lastly, you need to do a comprehensive map for the implementation process. The yearly map is a month-by-month project plan for what meetings and activities will occur during each month in the first year of implementation. The map should include all steering committee meeting dates and key action completion dates. Develop this map as the last page of your formal Strategic Career and Life Planning document.

YEARLY COMPREHENSIVE MAP

1. When to finish your Strategic Life Plan? _____
   Steps to do it include:

What?	Who?	By When?
1.		
2.		
3.		
4.		
5.		

2. Who to involve in your Parallel Process as "devil's advocates" for you?

Who?	How to Involve Them?
1.	
2.	
3.	
4.	

3. One-half to one day follow-up Formal Change Steering Committee Meetings:
   a. How frequent? _____
   b. Dates for next 12 months: _____ _____ _____ _____
   c. Who attends? _____
   d. Location: _____

4. Informal monthly reviews on the _____ of each month.
                                            1st, 2nd, 3rd, 4th   Saturday, Sunday, etc.

5. Weekly reviews at _____ am/pm each week on _____ (day).
   Make up 3 x 5 cards on vision/top priority actions.

6. Annual Strategic Life Review (and Plan Update):
   Which month? _____
   Location? _____
   # of days? _____
   With whom? _____
   _____
   _____

Annual Strategic Reviews

Conducting an Annual Strategic Review and Update of your Strategic Career and Life Plan is similar to a yearly independent financial audit. The annual review should include the following three main tasks:

1. Reacting to changes in the environment and implications for updating your core strategies.
2. Updating annual action plan priorities for the next 12 months.
3. Updating your yearly map.

The goal of the Annual Strategic Review and Update is to assess the status of the strategic career and life plan achievement itself.

Check with your tax accountant to see whether you can write off all or part of your annual review expenses. Going to a nice resort or wilderness retreat is a creative and freeing way to conduct proper Strategic Career and Life Planning. Take your trusty laptop computer to write the plan and use the computer's date/time stamp to document the work. This meeting may qualify as a legitimate tax write-off if your planning incorporates some "for profit" business that these expenses can be applied against. Again, consult with your tax preparer.

Summary: A Challenge for the Future

> *"To attain knowledge, add things every day. To obtain wisdom, remove things every day."*
>
> —Lao Tze

In these turbulent times, it is easy to feel powerless and a victim of circumstances. This Systems Thinking approach to Strategic Career and Life Planning is all about helping each person in your family or group feel empowered and be empowered.

Strategic Career and Life Planning is the right step toward defining and implementing the tough choices that are required in order to be successful and fulfilled in today's revolutionary global environment. To avoid tough choices is to let the future health and performance of your career and lifestyle be determined by circumstances that are increasingly beyond your control.

The ABCD pre-work, planning, implementing, and updating steps you have just completed give you a Strategic Life Management System for the daily management of your job, career, and life.

Success

To laugh often and much;
To win the respect of intelligent people and the affection of children;
To earn the appreciation of honest critics and endure the betrayal of false friends;
To appreciate beauty;
To reflect on and respect nature;
To find and foster the best in others;
To leave the world a bit better, whether by a healthy child, a garden patch, or a redeemed social condition;
To know even one life has breathed easier because you have lived.
This is to have succeeded.

—Author Unknown

PART 5

Appendix

> "*The future belongs to those who believe in their dreams.*"
>
> —Eleanor Roosevelt

This appendix contains the Career and Life Plan for Steve Haines, the author of this book, and his wife and business/life partner, Jayne.

Our Vision

Our vision is an intimate, healthy, happy, and prosperous life together.

"We will make a positive difference in our own lives...the lives of each other, our family including our grandson, Sebastian (born December 2, 1999)...and the lives of the primary people with whom we come in contact."

Our Mission

Our purpose or reason for being is to "make a difference" through our existence, in the following ways:

1. Caring for each other and ourselves with love, sharing, intimacy, learning, and support in all aspects of our lives (e.g., body, mind, emotions and spirit).

2. Sharing with our family and close friends our love, caring, support, time, and celebration of life in mutually enjoyable ways.

3. Assisting clients and Centre Members in the definition and achievement of their Visions.

Our Core Values

As the way we live our lives while "making a difference"

1. Integrity

Honesty, directness, and integrity in all our relationships.

2. Sharing

A caring, service, and abundance orientation with others.

3. Learning

Systems Thinking and continuous life-long learning as a way of life.

4. Service

High-quality professionalism and service (go the extra mile).

5. Environmental Awareness

Be environmentally sensitive and responsive in all we do.

6. Spirituality

Belief in the basic goodness of the human spirit and the presence of God in our lives.

7. Simplicity

Clarify and simplify the way we live our lives.

8. Fitness

Fitness and health as a basic daily foundation for living.

Our Key Success Factors (Goals)

The quantifiable measurements of our vision, mission, and values on a year-by-year basis to ensure continual improvement towards achieving our Personal Ideal Future Vision.

1. **Healthy**

2. **Prosperous**

3. **Honesty/Integrity**

4. **Sharing our abundance**

5. **High-quality professionalism and service**

6. **Proactive strategic life management**

7. **Travel and celebrate life**

8. **Simplicity**

Steve and Jayne's Strategic Life Plan: Yearly Report

Goals	1992 Baseline	1994 Target / Actual	1995 Target / Actual	1996 Target / Actual	Intermediate Targets 1997 Target / Actual	1998 Target / Actual	1999 Target / Actual	Target 2000 Target / Actual
1. Healthy: a. Body at proper weight & in shape/ fit–exercise/ walk 3x/week b. Spiritual fitness - church attendance - 2x/mo - 24x/yr								
2. Prosperous: a. Fees: (cash basis) b. Work: 10 -12 days/mo max 120 144/yr max w/ 144 target c. Materials Revenue: d. CSM royalties								
3. Truth, Honesty, Integrity: a. Self-Observation: critical incidents check 1/qtr by us b. Survey: feedback (include service/ quality)—Clients								
4. Make a Difference (Sharing Abundance): Money: a. Church Giving b. Donations each year • Elizabethtown • Environment • Vets (cash/non-cash)								

Steve and Jayne's Strategic Life Plan: Yearly Report

Goals	1992 Baseline	| Intermediate Targets |					Target 2000
		1994 Target|Actual	1995 Target|Actual	1996 Target|Actual	1997 Target|Actual	1998 Target|Actual	1999 Target|Actual	Target|Actual

Time:
  c. Give professional time (6 days/yr)
  d. Quality time with family: Moms, sister, daughter

5. High-quality professional/CSM assistance to others:
  a. Materials developed/quality (include books/Train-the-Trainer)
  b. 5 preferred clients & limit others
  c. Workshop delivery/marketing platforms
    • public/2 weeks of courses
    • Canada—Banff/Edmonton
    • US/TEC
    • International
    • San Diego
  d. Exhibits
  e. Newsletter/Web Tips
  f. Key Note Speaking (4$^+$ yr/increase)
    PF, ODN, ASTD, HR & San Diego Associations
  g. CSM Alliance/licenses (build #)
    • US
    • Canadian
    • International

Steve and Jayne's Strategic Life Plan: Yearly Report

Goals	1992 Baseline	| 1994 Target | Actual |	| 1995 Target | Actual |	| 1996 Target | Actual |	| 1997 Target | Actual |	| 1998 Target | Actual |	| 1999 Target | Actual |	| Target 2000 | Actual |
6. Proactive Life Strategic Management: a. Continuous Learning: one formal event/yr each b. Travel less-6 nights Mo w/o Jayne c. Intimate/Happy d. Strategic Planning for us & CSM e. Complete Ed.D. work f. Decide where to live/55 + retirement								
7. Travel & Celebrate Life: a. 2 season tickets & invite friends b. entertain friends/CSM once quarter/small once year/big - off season c. 2 East Coast visits/yr d. Travel: big trips/us 1/Christmas New Years 1/summer e. Travel: smaller trips -1 w/mom(s)/ NJ Shore f. Moms to San Diego 2/yr								
8. Simplicity: a. no debts b. finish all three books								

Core Strategies

Strategy 1: **Healthy**

Become fit and healthy in body, mind, and spirit (e.g., change to a healthy lifestyle).

Strategy 2: **Finances**

Continue to move towards a prosperous and independently wealthy financial state.

Strategy 3: **Professional services**

Be of service to others with high-quality and professional services.

Strategy 4: **Sharing abundance**

Make a difference through sharing our abundance.

Strategy 5: **Integrity**

Continually assess our integrity and honesty (e.g., all values).

Strategy 6: **Proactive**

Proactively plan and manage our lives and strategic life plan (i.e., a strategic management system) to ensure our vision is achieved on an ongoing basis.

Strategy 7: **Celebrate life**

Travel and celebrate life with each other, family, and friends.

Actions

Strategy 1: Healthy (life)

Become fit and healthy in body, mind, and spirit (e.g., change to a healthy lifestyle).

actions: (* = top priority)

Lead	Activity
Steve	*1. Exercise, walk, or do recreational activity 5 of 7 days (½ in AM-½ PM). Exercise at night on the road (30 minutes) and in AM for JH.
Jayne	*2. Lose 1 pound a week—until weight goal is achieved.
Both	*3. Eat properly including: • eat breakfast • reduce intake of fats • reduce intake of sugar, salt, meat, alcohol • reduce portion size and eat only until not hungry rather than full • have "healthy choice meals" at home plus Slim Fast • eat properly on the road
Steve	4. Continue Mondays without client work (max 4 days/wk with client work max 10 days/mo with clients @ $3,000/day). Stay away from weekend client work/travel (3 out of 4).
Jayne	5. Attend church service/event 2 times a month. Attend several other churches to determine if we should change.
Both	6. Share our lives intimately at a spiritual and physical level on an ongoing basis.

Actions

Strategy 2: Finances (life/business)

Continue to move towards a prosperous and independently wealthy financial state.

actions: (* = top priority)

Lead	Activity
Steve	*1. Steve works 10 full billable days a month (maximum) with clients; 120 days a year max + workshops and international work.
Steve	*2. Product Development: -write LOB#2 book (2001) -write strategy book (2002) -develop instrument/best practice package -have all eight volumes with shell built in
Steve	3. Fully develop LOB #2 Practice Area with other CSM members.
Jayne	*4. Update insurance records.
Steve	5. Hook up with an alliance roll-up-cash out some (2002)

Actions

Strategy 3: Professional services (business)

Be of service to others with high-quality and professional services.

actions: (* = top priority)

Lead	Activity
Steve	*1. Keep office automation current. - Do all business electronically - Volume VIII-Workbook 35 converted to MS Word - Steve fully functional on email/Internet (office and road)
Steve	*2. Have 5 preferred (i.e. long-term clients) per year with yearly maps for each and limit others.
Steve	*3. Develop the practice of the People Edge.
Steve	*4. Build San Diego awareness, clientele, visibility
Steve	*5. Once Systems Thinking book is published, go for keynote speaking as part of our practice.
Steve	*6. Investigate how to finish doctorate.
Steve	7. Decide on where to exhibit each year and which CSM members to join us each time (need 3 to 4 Partners at each in order to visit) -Linkage's Systems Thinking Conference
Steve	8. Products and Services Guide for Systems Thinking Press/market it, sell more.
Jayne	9. Use more recycled materials in products.
Steve	10. Office nearby? Decide in two years.
Steve	11. Develop CD-ROM products.
Steve	12. Perfect International Program.

Actions

Strategy 4: **Sharing abundance (life and business)**

Make a difference through sharing our abundance.

actions: (* = top priority)

Lead	Activity
Jayne	1. Give money each week to the church.
Jayne	2. Give to other charities, i.e., our alma maters, environment, veterans.
Steve	3. Limit pro bono or work for minimum professional fees to six days a year (two to three clients a year).
Steve	*4. Assist other Centre members with building their practices.
Jayne	5. Share our life plan with others.
Steve	6. Set up strategic alliances with other delivery firms as needed—The Ken Blanchard Companies, Human Technology Performance, WesCorp, and Virtual CEO.

Actions

Strategy 5: **Integrity (business)**

Continually assess our integrity, honesty, and environmental commitment (e.g., all values).

actions: (* = top priority)

Lead	Activity
Steve	*1. Quarterly self-assessments at Strategic Change Leadership Steering Committee meetings.
Steve	2. Self-assess quality of work with each client visit (do weekly).
Jayne	*3. Review KSFs/goals quarterly at Strategic Change Leadership Steering Committee offsite retreat location.
Steve	*4. Send customer satisfaction survey to select clients at end of each engagement.
Steve	5. Be open to feedback each day Steve works with clients (e.g., continue, more of, less of, plus consider informal feedback as a gift).
Jayne	6. In addition to using more recycled materials in products, reuse paper for scratch pads or to print draft documents.
Jayne	7. Continue to recycle products in both home and office: paper, plastics, cans, glass, print cartridges, paint, etc.

Actions

Strategy 6: Proactive (life and business)

Proactively plan and manage our lives and strategic life plan (i.e., a strategic management system) to ensure our vision is achieved on an ongoing basis.

actions: (* = top priority)

Lead	Activity
Both	1. Each of us goes to one learning event a year.
Steve	*2. Steve travel less—plan out each month • 6 days a month away from Jayne • almost no work or travel on weekends • Jayne travel with Steve 6 times a year.
Steve	*3. Quarterly meetings to review this plan—stay on track: April, July, and October.
Jayne	*4. Yearly planning review cycle (including year-end review) offsite each December/January.
Jayne	5. Simplify our lives—less consumption, more time together. Fewer material possessions purchased.
Jayne	6. Deposit money each month into Schwab One Account for vacations and taxes.
Both	7. Give presents of time, vacations instead of art, things, and stuff (less material consumption).
Steve	8. Re-do decks
Steve	9. Have hall closet re-fitted and dye or replace carpet—paint interior of house.
Steve	10. Plan international travels one year in advance.

Actions

Strategy 7:   Celebrate life (life)

Travel and celebrate life with each other, family, and friends.

actions: (* = top priority)

Lead	Activity
Steve	1. Season tickets to Chargers and share with friends.
Steve	2. Season Tickets to Padres and share with friends.

Both	3. Entertain friends at home twice a year plus one big event:
	   -USNA 1968/CSM
	    - Other

Jayne	*4. East Coast visits to see family (twice a year)
	   -Spring
	   -Fall
	   -January (Lois' 80th Birthday)

Steve	*5. Big trips by us (one a year in November or December/July-September)
Both	6. Other smaller trips—targets of opportunity
Jayne	*7. West Coast Mom visits (twice a year for both).
Steve	*8. Once a year rental at NJ Shore to see Moms/Linda and Family

Both	9. Spend quality time with family (see Key Success Factors and Travel for details):
	   • monthly with Monica/Pierre or Monica/Steve
	   • New England trip with Lois and Virginia

Steve	10. Go sailing in San Diego twice a year.

Implementation Game Plan

1. Quarterly meetings at a weekend retreat to review this plan. Stay on track: April, July, and October.

2. Yearly planning review cycle offsite (December) location TBD.

3. Year-end review January.

Now Available From

THOMSON COURSE TECHNOLOGY

Books • Videos • CD-ROMs • Computer-Based Training Products

If you enjoyed this book, we have great news for you. There are over 200 books available in the *Crisp Fifty-Minute™ Series*. For more information contact

Course Technology
25 Thomson Place
Boston, MA 02210
1-800-442-7477
www.courseilt.com

Subject Areas Include:

Management
Human Resources
Communication Skills
Personal Development
Marketing/Sales
Organizational Development
Customer Service/Quality
Computer Skills
Small Business and Entrepreneurship
Adult Literacy and Learning
Life Planning and Retirement